# FEEDING THE WORLD
# Meat

# Feeding the World

CORN

DAIRY PRODUCTS

EGGS

FARMED FISH

MEAT

RICE

SOY BEANS

WHEAT

# FEEDING THE WORLD

# Meat

### JANE E. SINGER

**MASON CREST**

Mason Crest
450 Parkway Drive, Suite D
Broomall, PA 19008
www.masoncrest.com

Printed and bound in the United States of America.

First printing
9 8 7 6 5 4 3 2 1

Series ISBN: 978-1-4222-2741-1
ISBN: 978-1-4222-2746-6
ebook ISBN: 978-1-4222-9078-1

The Library of Congress has cataloged the

hardcopy format(s) as follows:

       Library of Congress Cataloging-in-Publication Data

Singer, Jane E.
  Meat / Jane E. Singer.
     p. cm. — (Feeding the world)
  ISBN 978-1-4222-2746-6 (hardcover) — ISBN 978-1-4222-2741-1 (series) — ISBN 978-1-4222-9078-1 (ebook)
 1. Meat—Juvenile literature. 2. Food supply—Juvenile literature. I. Title. II. Series: Feeding the world.
 TX371.S56 2014
 641.3'6—dc23
                  2013004740

Publisher's notes:
The websites mentioned in this book were active at the time of publication. The publisher is not responsible for websites that have changed their addresses or discontinued operation since the date of publication. The publisher will review and update the website addresses each time the book is reprinted.

# CONTENTS

# CHAPTER ONE

# Where Does Meat Come From?

**T**he next time you sit down to eat, think about your food first. How did it get to your plate? Where did that food come from?

You might say, "the grocery store," or, "the refrigerator." Those answers are only sort of true. Yes, your food might come from the fridge. Your family bought it in a grocery store. But what about before that?

All food starts from somewhere before it ever gets to the grocery store. In fact, most food has a long story to tell.

## FARMS

Almost all food starts out on a farm. Farms are where food is grown or raised.

Vegetables and fruits are plants. Plants grow in the ground on farms. Farmers must pick the fruits and vegetables.

Grains are plants too. Grains include foods like rice and oats. They are tiny seeds from some kinds of plants. Grains grow in the ground on farms, just like fruits and vegetables.

Meat comes from animals. So do dairy products and eggs. Dairy **products** are anything that is made out of animal milk, like butter and cheese. All those animals are raised on farms too. They eat corn, grass, and other plants that grow in the ground.

## GROWING A GARDEN

If you really want to see where food comes from, try growing it yourself! Ask your parents if you can start a garden in your yard. Or grow some vegetables in pots if you don't have room for a whole garden. When you grow a garden, you'll see what happens to fruits and vegetables from start to finish. First, you plant seeds. They grow into tiny seedlings when they get water and sunlight. Then they keep growing bigger and bigger until they produce vegetables and fruits. Then you can harvest them and eat them. And you know just where they came from!

# FACTORIES

What about cereal and juice and frozen pizzas? Those things didn't grow on plants!

That might be true, but think about what those foods are made out of. The **ingredients** in cereal and juice and frozen pizzas come from farms.

Let's think about a frozen pizza. What is it made out of? First, there's the dough. The dough is made out of flour, which is crushed wheat. Wheat is a kind of grain.

Pizza sauce is made out of tomatoes. Tomatoes are a vegetable that grows on farms. The sauce might also have herbs in it, which are plants we use to flavor things.

Your pizza also has cheese on top. Cheese is a dairy product. Dairy products are made out of milk.

**8** **Meat**

All the meat you eat has a story. That story begins on a farm and ends with you eating your food. Meat doesn't come straight from the supermarket!

On top, the pizza might have some mushrooms and peppers. Both are vegetables that grow on farms.

Your frozen pizza might have pepperoni on it. Pepperoni is meat. It comes from pork and beef. In other words, it is made from pig and cow meat. Pigs and cows are raised on farms.

All of those ingredients go to the factory. The wheat comes from a grain farm. The tomatoes, mushrooms, and peppers come from vegetable farms. The milk for the cheese comes from a dairy farm. The meat for the pepperoni comes from animal farms.

The factory takes all of those ingredients and makes them into a pizza. Big machines grind all of the wheat into flour. Then they mix the flour with water and other stuff to make the dough. Other machines heat up the milk and add ingredients to it so the milk becomes cheese. Other parts of factories cut the vegetables and make the pepperoni.

At the end, all the ingredients are made into a pizza. It's ready for the next step.

## STORES

Now your food has to go to the grocery store. Lots of foods are sent to grocery store warehouses first. Warehouses keep food until it's ready to be sent to the store.

Farmers work hard to raise the animals we eat as meat. Raising animals can be difficult. Farmers have to make sure their animals get the right food and stay healthy. They also have to think about where to sell their animals and for how much.

 **10** **Meat**

## FARMERS' MARKETS

Sometimes a food's story looks a little different. Some farmers like to sell what they grow right to people who buy it. These farmers don't send their food to factories or to grocery stores. One way for farmers to sell their food is at farmers' markets. Lots of farmers get together. They set up stands. Then customers come shop for the food they need. They can talk to the farmers. They know where their food is coming from. Farmers' markets can sell all sorts of things. Some farmers sell fruits and vegetables. Some sell meat. Some make cheese or bread and sell that.

Trucks, planes, trains, and boats pick up food from factories. They take the food to warehouses.

At the warehouse, people sort all the food. Some of it will be sent to a grocery store in one area. Some will be sent to a grocery store a few miles away. More will be sent to other grocery stores in other places.

Then, trucks come and pick up the food at the warehouse. They take it to grocery stores.

This is the part you're probably familiar with already. If you've been to a grocery store, you know how it's all set up. You could probably find the meat in the store. Customers like you and your family buy the food they need. But they might not know just how far that food has come!

## FOCUSING ON MEAT

Lots of people don't know where meat comes from. Simply put, it comes from animals. We have to kill animals in order to eat them. Beef comes from cow. Pork comes from pig. Chicken, of course, comes from chicken.

When people find out that meat comes from animals, it can be scary. Some people don't like that meat used to be an animal.

But meat is something that we eat. It's a normal part of eating. (Some people choose not to eat meat, and that's okay too.)

In some parts of the world, it's easy to see that meat comes from animals. Grocery stores sell whole chickens and ducks with all their parts. Or they sell parts of animals that still look like animals.

## Where Does Meat Come From? 11

Almost all the food in the grocery store has ingredients that came from a farm in some way.

## 12 Meat

If you raise your own animals and make your own meat, then it's clear where it comes from! Lots of people around the world raise their own animals for meat.

In other parts of the world, meat doesn't really look like animals. It comes ground up or cut into pieces. It's packaged into plastic trays and wrapped up with plastic.

Farmers are in charge of raising the animals we eat. Some farmers raise sheep or goats. Some raise cows or buffalo. Others raise pigs. Farmers also raise chickens, geese, and ducks. Farmers have to feed their animals. They have to take care of them when they're sick.

When animals are fully grown, farmers send them to be killed for meat. Killing animals for meat is also called processing.

After they are killed, the animals are meat. People and machines cut up the meat into pieces. Then it's put into packages and sent to grocery stores.

Now you know where meat comes from. But there's a lot more to find out!

## VEGETARIANS

People who don't eat meat are called vegetarians. People don't eat meat for a lot of reasons. Some don't like that we have to kill animals to eat them. They think that we should be kind to all animals, and that means not eating them. Other vegetarians stop eating meat because they think it's healthier. For some people, not eating meat makes them feel better. Many people around the world are vegetarians. It's up to you whether you eat meat or not!

# CHAPTER TWO

# The History of Meat

eat is found in food all over the globe. People in Asia eat meat. People in North America eat meat. So do people in Africa. All around the world people eat meat.

We know that people have been eating meat for a long time. But just how long? Scientists think they've figured it out.

## THE FIRST MEAT EATER

It turns out that we have probably been eating meat for as long as people have been around. Not everyone agrees, but that's what the most recent clues say.

Scientists have found what they think is proof that our **ancestors** were eating meat over 3 million years ago!

People found very old animal bones in Ethiopia. They had cuts on them from stone tools.

Without fire, people couldn't cook the meat they ate. Instead, they ate it raw. Cooking with fire changed the way people ate meat and other food.

**16     Meat**

That meant that people had used tools to cut meat off of the bones. And people wouldn't have done that unless they were going to eat the meat.

For a long time, we only ate raw meat. Raw meat isn't cooked. People hadn't learned how to build fires to cook their food yet.

Later on, we did learn how to use fire. No one knows exactly when or how. But after that, we could cook our meat and other food. Meat was a lot easier for our bodies to take in when it was cooked. That's when meat eating as we know it was born.

# SMARTER PEOPLE?

Meat eating might have even made humans smarter. Before we started eating meat, we just ate plants. We had to eat a lot of plants to get enough energy to stay healthy.

We had to have big **digestive systems**—big stomachs and intestines. Our digestive systems had to be really good at getting energy from plants. If they weren't, we wouldn't have lived very long!

After a while, we learned that we could eat meat. Meat has more energy in it. Our digestive systems didn't have to be so big. They didn't have to be as good at getting energy out of our food.

Instead of a big digestive system, we got bigger brains. Our digestive systems got smaller as our brains got bigger. All that extra energy we got from meat made our brains bigger.

Bigger brains meant smarter people. We learned how to use tools. We made languages to speak and write to each other. We built houses. We became modern-day people!

# RAISING ANIMALS

Even though people were eating meat, we didn't have farms yet. Thousands of years ago, people had to hunt for their food. They hunted wild animals. No one knew how to raise a cow for meat.

Then people figured out it would be a lot easier if they could just train animals to live near them. When hunting, you had to be lucky to eat. You had to find the right animals and kill them. You might not always get so lucky. Then you might go hungry.

If you could train animals to live near you, you knew you would always have meat. You

Sheep and goats were the first animals people raised on farms. Once people began farming, hunting and finding food was less important. More and more people could also choose what they wanted to eat.

wouldn't have to search for them in the wild. You wouldn't go hungry!

Taking wild animals and teaching them to live on a farm is called domestication. As people domesticated animals, the animals became less dangerous. For example, wild wolves could hurt people. But once people trained them, over time they became dogs. Dogs that live with people are much less dangerous than wild wolves!

People started raising animals at least 10,000 years ago. That's a long time ago. Sheep and goats were some of the first animals that people started raising. Sheep and goats were domesticated in the

**18** **Meat**

Middle East thousands of years ago.

Next, cows and pigs were domesticated. Cows were domesticated in western Asia. Pigs were domesticated in China. People all over the world were figuring out how to train animals to live on farms.

Chickens came next. People in India domesticated wild jungle fowl. The jungle fowl became the chicken we know today. That was 2,000 years ago.

Today we have a lot of animals that we raise for meat. Most of them live all over the world. You can find chickens in India. But you can also find them in Latin America, Australia, and more places.

## MORE THAN JUST MEAT

Animals do a lot more for us than just give us meat. We make clothes out of animals. Wool comes from cutting hair off sheep. Leather is cow skin. We make glue out of hooves. We get milk from cows, goats, sheep, and more. We can ride horses and camels to get places. In the past, animals did even more. They helped us do work on farms. They pulled carriages to help us get around. Domesticating animals was one of the best ideas people have ever had!

# CHAPTER THREE

# Who Raises the Meat We Eat?

**F**armers are in charge of raising animals for meat. They have a lot to do to make sure their animals are big and healthy. Taking care of animals is hard work.

Farmers are the ones who take care of animals. They feed them. They take care of them when they're sick. They make sure they don't run away from the farm.

## BIG FARMER, SMALL FARMER

Not every farmer is the same. There are farmers who have big farms. There are farmers who have small farms.

Farmers with big farms raise hundreds or thousands of animals. Some chicken farms raise over a million birds!

Some farms have hundreds or even thousands of animals. Small family farms might have just a few. Today, many big farms raise animals close together. Not everyone agrees that raising animals like this is a good idea.

## 22    Meat

Big farms are sometimes huge fields. There are many cows or sheep walking around. They are kept in with fences.

Sometimes the farm is a bunch of barns. The animals are raised in the barns. They don't go outside. Pigs and chickens are often raised that way.

Usually only one kind of animal lives on a big farm. The farm focuses on raising cows or pigs. It doesn't grow any vegetables. It doesn't raise any other kinds of animals.

On big farms, there's probably more than one farmer. There may be lots and lots of farmworkers. They all share the job of taking care of the animals.

Other farms are a lot smaller. The farmer only raises a few animals. She might have a herd of 15 cows or 30 sheep.

Small farms are run by one or two farmers and some farmworkers. They help the farmer earn money. The farm sells meat to other people.

Some farms are even smaller! Lots of families around the world only have one or two animals. One water buffalo can give a family a lot of milk. And it can give birth to more buffalos that the family can eat.

Tiny farms might only have ten chickens, or a couple of goats. These farms might have just enough to feed a family. If there were more animals, it would be too hard to take care of them all. These farms don't often sell meat to other people.

Water buffalo are kind of like cows. People raise them for milk and meat. Most of the water buffalo in the world are raised in India and other parts of Asia.

 **Who Raises the Meat We Eat?** **23**

Farmers must make sure to feed their animals well. Healthy animals make better meat than sick animals, so farmers must work hard to keep their animals from getting ill.

**24**   **Meat**

China raises more pigs for meat than any other country in the world. Pork (meat from pigs) is a big part of Chinese cooking.

# FACTORY FARMS

What do you picture when you think of the word "farm"? Do you think of grassy fields and sunshine and barns? That isn't how farms always look. Some huge farms are actually more like factories. All of the animals are inside. There are lots of machines. That's why they're called factory farms. Most of the animals we eat were in a factory farm at some point in their lives. Some animals live in a factory farm for their whole lives. Some live there only at the end of their lives, when they're adults.

# COUNTRY BY COUNTRY

People in pretty much every country in the world raise animals for meat. But some countries raise more animals than others.

The country that raises the most meat is China. There are really big farms in China. They **produce** millions of animals for meat.

## Who Raises the Meat We Eat? 25

Farmers aren't the only people who help raise animals. Veterinarians are doctors for animals. They work with farmers when an animal is sick.

**26** **Meat**

China raises a lot of pigs and produces a lot of pork. China produces over 50 million tons of pork, in fact. That's a lot of meat!

The United States produces the second-largest amount of meat in the world. The United States also has huge farms with many animals. Brazil also produces a lot of meat. After the United States, Brazil is the third-biggest meat producer in the world.

These countries send a lot of meat to other parts of the world. India sends one and a half million tons of buffalo meat to other countries. Brazil sends away almost half of all the meat that it produces.

## WHO EATS THE MOST MEAT?

In 2012, the country that ate the most meat in the world per person was Luxembourg. That's a tiny country in the middle of Europe. Each person there ate on average about 300 pounds (136.5 kilograms) of meat every year. The United States came in second. People in India eat the least meat. They only ate around 7 pounds per person.

# CHAPTER FOUR

# How Is Meat Raised?

It takes a lot to raise an animal. A farmer has to keep it healthy when it's a baby. A farmer has to know what to feed it. She has to give it medicine when it's sick.

Most of all, a farmer needs patience. Animals can take a long time to grow up. Vegetables grow a lot faster. You can plant lettuce in the ground and pick it a month later. With animals, you have to wait many months, or even years before you can eat them.

## CHICKENS

Chickens are one of the smallest animals we eat often. They are birds.

Chickens often live inside their whole lives. They are raised on really big farms with thousands of other chickens.

It's easier to raise chickens if they're inside. Farmers don't have to worry about other animals like coyotes or bears eating them. And farmers with big farms want to keep their chickens all together.

Many farms raise chickens inside in places like this. Farmers feed their chickens food called mash. Mash is made from soybeans, corn, and small grains.

 **30** **Meat**

Many farms that raise chickens buy chicks from hatcheries. A hatchery is a special kind of farm that raises baby chickens. Hatcheries help eggs to hatch and make sure the chicks are healthy. Then, hatcheries sell chicks to other farms.

Farmers usually buy chicks (baby chickens) from companies. There are special farms that hatch eggs into chicks. You can actually order them on the Internet and in catalogs. Then those companies ship chicks through the mail.

The chicks have to be kept warm and safe. They are weak and can get sick easily. They have to be kept in small, warm boxes. They can't just wander around outside.

The chicks grow for a few weeks. They lose their soft fluff and grow feathers. Their legs get longer. They start to look like adult chickens.

Farmers feed chickens something called mash. Mash has grain in it. It has corn. Sometimes it has soybean oil. The mash is supposed to give the chickens the right balance of the things they need to eat to stay healthy.

Giving chickens good food means the chickens will taste better. Farmers want to make sure their chickens get good food.

Goats were one of the first animals people raised on farms. Today, goats are raised for meat and milk around the world.

**32**   **Meat**

# COWS

Cows usually spend most of their lives outside. They wander around in herds and eat grass. The farmer will give them extra food if he needs to.

The farmer has to keep her cows fenced in. If there were no fences, the cows might try to run away from the farm!

A herd of cows is made up mostly of female cows and babies. There might be one or two male cows, called bulls.

Each year, the female cows give birth. Some of the babies might become meat after some time.

Baby cows are called calves. They are usually kept with their mothers. They drink their mothers' milk and start to grow up. After a while, the calves learn to eat grass like an adult cow.

On other farms, calves are split up from their mothers. They are raised in **pens**. People feed them. Most cows growing up away from their mothers are raised to give milk.

When they're old enough, cows are sold. They are taken to a place where someone comes to look at them. Or people who want to buy cows come to the farm.

The people who buy the cows take them to a feedlot. Feedlots are places where cows and other animals are given lots of food so they gain a lot of weight. A heavy animal can turn into more meat than a skinny one.

Cows can get sick, just like people. Small farmers can keep a close eye on their cows. They can see if one gets sick. Then they can give it medicine or keep it away from the other cows.

Farmers with bigger farms and the people who run feedlots have a harder time keeping animals from getting sick. There are lots of cows packed tightly together. Sickness can spread fast. Some farms might have a **veterinarian** to help with sick cows.

# GOATS

Goats spend their lives on farms. They usually live outside rather than inside in a barn or feedlot.

Lots of goats live on small farms. There aren't too many huge goat farms in the world. Families have a goat or two for milk and meat. Farmers who want to make money from goats might have a small herd of them.

Many people believe that raising animals on feedlots is wrong. They feel that animals raised on feedlots aren't treated well and aren't as healthy as other animals.

**34** **Meat**

Farmers have to make sure their goats are healthy. They need to give them a place to live all year round. If the farm is somewhere with cold weather, goats need a warm place to stay in the winter. Farmers have to treat sick goats. They can give them medicines depending on why they are sick.

Goats also need a lot of land to get food. Goats will eat just about anything. They'll eat grass and weeds. But they'll also eat vegetables, fruit, hay, and grain.

Goats are very smart. They can get out of lots of pens. The farmer has to be smarter. She has to figure out a way to keep her goats in one place. Fences are important to keep other animals out, too. **Predators** can eat goats.

# PIGS

People around the world eat pigs. Lots of the pigs we eat are raised inside. They live in big sheds or barns.

One big reason pigs are raised inside is because of temperature. Pigs can get overheated quickly. They can also get sunburned! If pigs are kept inside, farmers can control the temperature. They can make sure the pigs don't get too hot.

When piglets are born, they are kept with their mothers for a couple of weeks. Then they're put in their own area together.

Growing pigs get food that is mostly grain like corn or soybeans. It might also have meat in it. Pigs eat both vegetables and meat, just like us. With enough food, tiny piglets grow quickly. They end up as very big pigs!

Some countries keep pigs that are going to have babies in special tiny pens. They can't move much. The pens keep the pigs from hurting each other. These pens also let people raise more pigs in a small space.

Some countries have made laws against these small pens. The laws in these countries say that pigs should have more room to live so they can move around.

# DISAGREEMENTS ABOUT ANIMALS

Not everyone agrees with how animals are raised for meat. Some people think the way we raise animals is unkind. Some say we should be nicer to the animals we raise for food.

**How Is Meat Raised?** 35

Some farmers raise their animals in an organic way. Organic animal farmers let their animals walk around fields and have plenty of room. They don't feed their animals chemicals or feed that has been grown with chemicals.

## 36 Meat

Some people don't like feedlots, for example. Animals are crowded together in feedlots. They get sick easily. They don't eat the food that they're meant to. Some feedlots give their animals corn or soybeans even though their stomachs are made for eating grass or other plants. Cows and other animals in feedlots might not have very good lives.

There are other ways to raise animals. People have come up with a lot of ways to raise animals for food.

Many say that raising animals on small farms is better than raising them on big farms and feedlots. If farmers raise animals on small farms, they can pay more attention to them. They can let them eat grass. The animals don't get sick as often because they don't live so closely together.

**Organic** farms are another solution. Organic meat comes from animals that have been raised a certain way. They are fed with organic food that hasn't been grown with **chemicals**. They aren't given certain medicines that could be bad for people if we eat the meat from those animals. People who buy organic meat think it's healthier for them and for the animals.

Other people think that meat is meat. They don't mind that some animals are raised on bigger farms or on feedlots.

Some might also be thinking about money. Meat from big farms and feedlots often costs less. Organic meat and meat from small farms can cost a lot of money. People can't eat as much meat if they don't have enough money to buy it.

Raising animals for food can be a tricky thing. There are lots of things to think about and many choices to make. Should you eat meat that only comes from small farms? Should you eat meat at all? It's up to you! But learning about meat is the first step to making up your mind.

## ORGANIC

Have you heard the word "organic" before? It means that something is made without chemicals. For meat, it means the farmer didn't use chemical pesticides to kill bugs or chemical fertilizers to grow the animals' feed. Organic farmers want to avoid using chemicals that could poison the ground, animals, and people.

# CHAPTER FIVE

# How Does Meat Get to Your Plate?

N ow that the animal you're going to eat is about to become meat, what happens next? It still has a long way to go to get to you.

## BECOMING MEAT

After animals are raised to be adults, it's time to start thinking about making them into meat. Animals must be killed before we can eat them as meat.

Different animals live longer before they're killed. Chickens are killed after they are six months old. Cows live longer, between one and two years.

Farmers usually have to send their animals to a place to be processed. There are special buildings that do it for them.

Places that process animals try to kill them quickly. Often, the animals will be knocked out first. That way, they aren't awake and won't feel anything.

People don't want to take home a whole cow or pig! Butchers take big pieces of meat and cut them up into smaller pieces.

# 40 Meat

Meat is often moved from the factory to the store in refrigerated trucks. These trucks keep the meat cold and make sure it's still good when it gets to the people who are going to buy it.

Animals are sent from farms to processing factories. Small farmers will usually send their animals to get processed somewhere else. One processing factory will take in animals from hundreds of farms.

Sometimes the animals are already there. If they have been sent to a feedlot, there might be a processing factory in the same place.

After the animals have been killed, they are meat. They are ready for the next steps to get to your plate.

# CLEANING UP

Fresh meat has to be cleaned up a little. Chickens, turkeys, and other birds have to be plucked. That means taking off the birds' feathers. Most people don't want feathers on their meat in the fridge.

Meat is washed off to get rid of blood and bacteria. All of the organs have to be taken out too.

Some animals are hung up for awhile. Beef, for example, hangs in a fridge for a week or so. It gets more flavor as it hangs.

**How Does Meat Get to Your Plate?** 41

Next time you eat meat from the grocery store, think about all the people who had to work hard to get you your food. Your food has a long story from the farm to the store!

**42 Meat**

# INSPECTING

Inspection is an important part of selling meat. Inspection means people look at the meat to make sure it's safe to eat. **Bacteria** can grow on meat. We can get sick when we eat meat that has bacteria on it.

Meat is inspected in the processing factories. Inspectors look at the meat to make sure the animal it came from wasn't sick.

Inspectors also look at where the meat is being processed. The whole place has to be clean. The animal cages have to be clean. The machines have to be clean.

The inspectors also send some meat to labs. They send meat to scientists. Then the scientists do tests on the meat. They make sure it doesn't have any bacteria or anything else we shouldn't eat in it.

# CUTTING

You don't normally see a whole pig or buffalo in the grocery store! Meat is cut up first before it gets to the store. In some countries, however, you might see a whole chicken or duck.

There are special ways to cut each kind of meat. Bacon comes from the sides and stomach of a pig. Brisket comes from the front part of a cow.

Butchers do the cutting. They know exactly how to cut meat and where each piece should come from.

Then the meat gets packaged up. Meat is often sold on trays and covered with plastic. That way, bacteria won't get in.

The packages have labels on them. The labels tell people what kind of meat it is. It says that the meat has been inspected. And it gives a date that the meat should be eaten by. Meat doesn't stay good forever, so people have to know when they need to eat the meat they buy.

# MORE FACTORIES

Some meat is sent to another factory. These factories make food out of meat. They make sausage. Or pepperoni. Or chicken nuggets.

Those factories take the meat they get and make it into a food with meat in it. There's a lot of chopping and mixing and adding other ingredients. At the end, the factories have made a new food.

# THE STORE

Finally, your meat is getting closer to you. Trucks will pick up the meat at the factories. Then they might bring them right to a warehouse. Or they might bring them to a boat or a plane. The meat could get sent around the world!

Grocery stores own the warehouses. They keep the food at warehouses until it's ready to go to the store.

At the warehouse, the meat gets sorted. Some of it will go to one grocery store. Some will go to another. The meat can get sent to lots and lots of different stores.

The grocery store gets the shipment of meat. Workers unload it and put it on shelves.

That's where you come in! You and your family come to the store. You go to the meat section and pick out what kind of meat you want. You have lots of choices.

The next time you go to the grocery store, think about your meat. It might not look like an animal, but that's where it came from. Think about who raised your meat. A lot of work went into it!

The package might even say where the meat is from. It could be from the other side of the country. Or it could be from a different country altogether.

Once you start thinking about where your food comes from, eating becomes more of an adventure!

# WORDS TO KNOW

**ancestors:** People related to us from an earlier time in history.

**bacteria:** Tiny creatures so small you can't see them. Some can make people sick, but most don't, and some even help keep people healthy.

**chemicals:** Artificial substances that farmers use to help their crops grow, but which might be poisonous to humans.

**digestive system:** The parts of your body (like your stomach) that allow you to eat food and get energy from it.

**ingredients:** Foods that are mixed with others to make new foods.

**organic:** Crops and animals grown without chemicals like pesticides (used to kill bugs).

**pens:** Spaces with fences on all four sides.

**predators:** Animals who hunt and eat other smaller or weaker animals.

**produce:** To make or gather to sell to others.

**products:** Things people make, buy, and sell.

**veterinarian:** A doctor for animals who helps farmers when animals get sick.

# FIND OUT MORE

## ONLINE

Farm Animals Around the World
www.enchantedlearning.com/coloring/farm.shtml

Kids' Health: Vegetarian
www.cyh.com/HealthTopics/HealthTopicDetailsKids.aspx?p=335&np=284&id=2238

Where Does This Food Come From?
www.1millionacts.com.au/inspiration/kids-quiz-where-does-this-food-come-from

## IN BOOKS

Gibbons, Gail. *The Vegetables We Eat*. New York: Holiday House, 2007.

Owen, Ruth. Meat: *Life on a Sheep Farm*. New York: Windmill Books, 2012.

Pollan, Michael. *The Ominvore's Dilemma (Young Reader's Edition)*. New York: Penguin, 2009.

# INDEX

## ABOUT THE AUTHOR

Jane E. Singer is a freelance writer with several titles to her name. Singer writes about health, history, and other topics that affect young people. She is passionate about learning in and out of the classroom.

## PICTURE CREDITS